The Complete Guide to Hiking with Babies and Toddlers

The New York City Metropolitan Area Edition

LORI LABORDE

Illustrations by
Zoë Bean

FLYING FINCH PRESS

A special thank you to my family and friends for making this book a reality. I am ever grateful for your support and encouragement.

Flying Finch Press. New Jersey
All rights reserved. Published 2019.
Printed in China

LaBorde, Lori, 1982-
The Complete Guide to Hiking with Babies and Toddlers:
New York City Metropolitan Area Edition/ by Lori LaBorde;
Illustrated by Zoë Bean
ISBN-978-0-692-11960-0
Book design and layout by Sweety

For
Remi Lou, Ethan, and Finch

Letter To Parents

There is little more beautiful to me, than watching parents connect with each other and their babies in nature. I believe that we have a real connection to the natural world—that by spending time there we can become calm, feel healed, and find our spirit renewed. And I cannot think of a better place to nurture the sacred bond between a parent and a child. Yet as a parent, I understand first-hand how difficult it can be to get out the door with a baby, let alone into the woods. This book is firmly rooted in the realism of parenthood, and will walk you through a holistic approach to broaden your connection with the environment while simultaneously becoming a safer and more apt hiker. Becoming a parent changed the way I saw and interpreted the world. When it came to the outdoors, I felt that I needed more resources than were available to me. In this book I share with you the stories, lessons, and practicalities I learned through my experiences guiding parents and babies on hikes throughout this region. So whether you are a novice hiker or an expert outdoor enthusiast, I hope you will find within these pages all of the resources you need to help you foster positive experiences, curiosity, and confidence when hiking with your young children.

Let's hit the trail!

Lori

Table of Contents

Introduction

As far back as I can remember I was drawn to nature. My childhood home had a small stretch of forest behind my house that we called "the woods," and I grew up exploring them. Even at a young age, I recognized that I found comfort in the sounds of the leaves moving in the wind, and in the little chipmunks that scurried into their little holes when they saw me coming. I found peace in the sunlight peeking at me through the treetops, and in the air that filled my lungs. One of my favorite homework assignments was when my first grade teacher had our class create binoculars out of toilet paper rolls and string and take an afternoon to observe birds in our backyards. My house sat along a main road, but our backyard stretched up a big grassy hill and at the top of the hill sat a huge oak tree that stood guardian to the woods. I remember sitting near the oak all by myself, with my binoculars in hand, observing and sketching one robin in particular. The robin would pop along the ground and then stop all of a sudden, as if to see if anyone had caught it doing something it shouldn't have been doing. I could have watched this robin all day—wondering what it would do next. After that, I started studying and tracing the pictures in my parents' <u>Book of North American Birds</u>, published by Reader's Digest.

My first attempts at nature photography were taken in the woods behind my house. It was taken on a purple plastic rectangle (I believe it was a Vivitar 110). The flash was an attachable vertical

piece of plastic that housed about eight one-time-use flashes, called a flip flash (one of the many exciting perks of being an '80s child). Nonetheless, my woods were inspiring. They were exciting and full of adventure, yet peaceful and calming. The woods made me feel free and this sense of freedom was important to me.

I spent as many days as I could in the woods. I couldn't get through a summer without coming down with itchy red rashes of Poison Ivy. One summer I had it so bad on my face that the doctor made me take steroids, and that was the quickest it ever went away. In college I finally took to becoming an expert at identifying the various ways that Poison Ivy appears—a tricky plant that one can be! Years later when I was pregnant, I was fortunate enough to spend my entire summer outdoors working as a naturalist at a summer camp. One of my first lessons with the campers was how to identify Poison Ivy and how to wash up properly if you had touched it.

The part of my first pregnancy that I remember most, was during the summer at the camp. It was lovely and relatively easy, and while it was the second trimester, I partially attribute this blissful period in my life to the fact that I was able to nurture the amazing life growing inside me while spending most of my time in the place that gave me the most peace and satisfaction—the outdoors. After my daughter was born I was eager to share my love of the outdoors with her. But suddenly, as a new mother, I was finding that there was so much that I doubted, about everything, let alone taking my baby into the woods. The baby gear, logistics, and what ifs were a huge hurdle to overcome and I came to the realization that if it was hard for someone like me to get on the trail with my daughter, surely others had similar hesitations.

A few months later, in 2014, I became a licensed hiking guide, through the New York State Department of Environmental Conservation. Since then, I have been leading parents with little ones on hikes, working to build their confidence and empower them to continue to hike on their own. Joining a guided hike is a wonderful way to ease into outdoor explorations with your babies—less planning, learning about places to go, and meeting a community of like-minded people. But for whatever reason, you may not always be able to join a group. It is my hope, that this easy-to-follow book will serve as your complete on-the-go hiking companion, so that you too can reap the many benefits that hiking with your children can bring.

Part One

Being a Steward
of the
Natural World

Chapter 1

Stewardship & Leave No Trace

If you are reading this book, you already hold a special place for nature in your heart. And as someone who cares about our natural spaces, it's important to understand that the practice of being good stewards of our environment begins as a state of mind. Our mind influences our thoughts, and our thoughts influence our actions. As our little ones watch us and grow, they too will practice what they learn from us. So, it is worthwhile to take a moment and ask ourselves these two questions:

How can I take responsibility for my actions and myself while I'm in nature?
In what ways can I help protect my natural world?

There isn't any one way to answer these questions. There is, however, an established code of ethics that can serve as a practical guide while on the trail. Hikers and outdoor enthusiasts practice the "Leave No Trace" principles to enjoy their time in nature while minimally impacting the environment.

There are seven widely accepted principles of Leave No Trace that pertain to hiking with infants and toddlers.

1. Plan Ahead and Prepare

Knowing where you are going, what the conditions are, and how long you will stay, will help you pack responsibly and reduce unnecessary bulk. Planning ahead and preparing will ensure that you have adequate clothing and food, as well as the proper waste management system (i.e. a ziplock bag for a day hike).

2. Travel and Camp on Durable Surfaces

Where there is a trail, stick to it. This will protect habitats even if it doesn't seem like protection measures are necessary. As stated above, practicing Leave No Trace is a state of mind. If you happen to venture into an area where there is no trail, have your group spread out to minimize compression to any one area.

3. Dispose of Waste Properly

It's important to not confuse the word "biodegradable" with Leave No Trace. This means that even that apple core you are tempted to toss must leave with you until you can dispose of it properly. If you are out for a day hike, this is easy: Take out everything you brought in—the biodegradable stuff, the diaper stuff, the foil, tissues, gum, etc. If you need to go to the "bathroom" while on a hike, or especially if you are camping, it's good to be aware of any state regulations that may apply, depending on where you are hiking. Distances may vary slightly from state to state, so I recommend the Boy Scouts of America code. Human waste should be buried in holes six to eight inches deep (called "catholes") located at least 200 feet from water, camp, or trails. Any wash water should also be discarded at this distance. The toilet paper stuff should be carried out with you. Back to the zip-lock idea—I like it because it seals!

Umm...what is 200 feet?

Imagining 200 feet may be difficult, so it is worth pacing out. Depending on your stride, 200 feet is equal to about 35 to 50 paces. A pace is a double step at natural stride. Start with your legs together and start to walk with your left foot. When your right foot hits the ground, that is a double step, or one pace. Another image to help estimate 200 feet is about five houses wide or about two-thirds of an American football field.

4. Leave What You Find

Be aware that it is illegal to collect pieces of nature on state and federal lands such as State Forests, National Forests, and Parks and Wilderness Areas. The regulations work to protect threatened or endangered species, limit transportation of invasive species, or reduce negative impacts on habitats. They are based on scientific data and remind us that while something may seem harmless, it may in fact be detrimental to the ecosystem. Wherever you may be, the 4th principle should encourage you to be mindful should you choose to take something home with you.

With this said, as a mother of little explorers, this poses a real tension that I am aware of. When my daughter started to hike on her own, she began to collect mementos. Whether it be a leaf, an acorn, or pocket full of pebbles, she was connecting with her world. Though I strongly support Leave No Trace, I want to encourage my children to connect with the natural world. I want them to be curious, I want them to feel something tangible in their hands, and to have a way to reflect about nature when we are home. Sometimes I feel that her "tokens of appreciation" can benefit nature in the long run—that by having a seed pod or flower bloom to look at when she's home, she can be reminded of the fun and freedom of the outdoors. And with that simple object, be more likely to grow an appreciation of nature and become an adult who feels a sense of responsibility and urgency to preserve and protect it. But there is a balance here that shouldn't be minimized, and certainly provides an opportunity to teach our children how to be a responsible steward.

5. Minimize Campfire Impacts

Here in the northeast, many of our natural areas are heavily trafficked. It is not unusual to see remnants of fire rings while hiking along a trail. You may have seen evidence of campfires—on the ground, on a large rock, surrounded by small stones, or even with logs hauled for seating. While it may seem harmless, moving logs or branches from their place of origin disrupts the habitats of living creatures. Soil is filled with important living organisms that contribute to the health of the ecosystem. The high heat intensity of a campfire sterilizes the soil, making regrowth a long process. While there is no denying the lure and nostalgia that only a campfire can bring, there are ways to responsibly build a campfire that work to leave no trace. To learn more about ways to build campfires that minimize negative impacts, see Appendix IV: Useful Resources.

6. Respect Wildlife

A colorful bird, a familiar birdsong, a frog's desperate leap for safety, or the stoic and silent stare of a buck—this is why we are here, right?! Run-ins with wildlife can be exciting because (for most of us) they don't happen every day. And while these moments may bring a feeling of being more in touch with our animal brethren and the natural world, it's important to remember that we are only visitors. Our presence alone can be disruptive to animal behavior and in some cases can jeopardize their normal discourse of life. So when we are stalling for that perfect photo opportunity or intentionally feeding an animal to get a closer look, we have to be mindful that to be good stewards means to not disrupt behavior or jeopardize breeding, foraging, or shelter. That empty nest in the cherry tree will be used again next spring.

7. Be Considerate of Others

This is simple. Your behavior on the trail affects the quality of others' experiences. Allow others to have the same quality experience that you hope to have.

Part Two

Planning and Preparation

Chapter 2

Safety Tips

Hiking with infants and toddlers is a more positive and safer experience when you have thoughtfully planned for your trip. This includes having a plan for how the actual hike will take place and end. As you prepare, you must account not only for your child's well-being, but also for your own. It's easy to discount the importance of self-care, but your child's safety depends on it. Let's get started.

Prep Before You Go

- ***What will the weather be like?***
  This will help you dress and pack appropriately. (*See Chapter 5: What Should I Wear?*)

- ***When is it too hot?***
  (~ 90° F) My doctor couldn't give me a definitive number, so I set my own limits. I found that 90 degrees and above was too hot to front-carry my daughter. Remember that your baby is feeling your body heat as well as their own. Ninety degrees is also a good limit for back-carrying, even if your carrier has a sun shade. Remember to think of yourself and the added stress of carrying an infant or toddler. It's easier to become dehydrated and feel faint or dizzy in extreme

weather. Ultimately you will find a comfortable range for what works for you and your child.

- ***When is it too cold?***
  ($< 20°$ F) As with warmer temperatures, you will find that there is a limit to when you will want to be out with your child. Factors you need to consider are the amount of time you will be outside as well as your gear (e.g. the type of jacket you are wearing, how you are carrying your child, and what materials you are using to layer your clothing). When I front-carried, I could be out in pretty cold temperatures ($\sim 20°$ F) if I was only staying out 30-60 minutes. Back-carring is different, because even in the best gear, your child's face will still be exposed. On days colder than 20 degrees I wasn't comfortable hiking with my child. It's good practice to remind yourself of what you are hoping to gain from your outdoor experience. Set an intention for your hike, as you would do in yoga. This way, you will be more likely to keep your outdoor experiences positive ones.

- ***Decide how long you want to be out.***
  This will help you pack an appropriate amount of food and dress accordingly.

- ***Who are you going with?***
  It's always best to go with another adult, just in case the unexpected happens. This is especially important when you are hiking with children. If your friend cancels last minute,

consider going another day.

- ***Do you have a map?***
  There are some really good map apps available these days. However, I never recommend relying solely on your phone, just in case you lose signal or your battery dies. (*Note: colder weather drains a battery faster.*)

- ***If you do not have a map, does someone in your party know the way?***
  Do not go for a hike with infants and toddlers if you do not have a map and you do not know the way.

- ***Do you know how to read your map?***
  (*Brush up on your skills in Chapter 10: Basic Map Reading*)

- ***Tell someone where you are going and when you expect to be back.***

- ***Pack food that you know is a winner!***
  This is not the time to explore textures and tastes with your infant or try something new with your picky toddler. Be sure to pack food and drinks they like, and bring enough for the way there, while on the trail, and the trip home. Snacks and meals that do not spoil are encouraged.

- ***Bring plenty of water.***
  A sippy cup of water (~8 oz.) for an infant or toddler is okay for a short day hike. Bring more in warmer weather and when you will be out

longer. Bring at least two bottles of water for yourself (at least 24 oz.). You will need extra water to stay hydrated while carrying your child. You may also want to leave a bottle of water in the car just for your ride to and from the hike.

- *Eat as you go.*
  Snacks for you are important to keep you happy and energized, even when on a short day hike. Remember to take all food scraps and garbage out with you.

- *Make sure your first aid kit is up to date.*
  You can purchase a pre-made first aid kit. These kits are great because they are compact in size and eliminate the guesswork of building your own. However, building your own first aid kit can be more cost effective because you can buy in bulk and refill when necessary. If you would like to put together your own, see Chapter 3 for a complete list of essentials when building your own first aid kit.

- *Be aware of potentially dangerous insects, wildlife, and plants that you may come into contact with, and know how to avoid them* (*See Appendix III: Avoiding Potential Dangers on the Hike*).

Safety on the Hike
- *Drink your water!*
  Sometimes it's easy to avoid drinking the water

28

you packed. But your body works better when hydrated. On colder days, drinking water will help your body maintain heat. It is best to pack your water in a convenient and easily accessible place. (*See tip in Chapter 3 to reduce your water weight and bulk.*)

- **Be flexible, be flexible, be flexible.**
  You may not get in those four miles you were hoping for, or reach the view. It's the whole experience that counts—the time together in nature, the fresh air, the nap, and the knowledge that you got yourself and your little one(s) outside.

- **If you encounter a wild animal...**
  Give it space and do not approach or attempt to feed it. Let it know you are there by blowing a whistle, clapping your hands, or by talking to it. Slowly move away from the animal without turning your back. (*See Appendix III: Avoiding Potential Dangers on the Hike.*)

- **If you think you or your child touched a poisonous plant...**
  Make a note of it and remember to wash with soapy water and a towel for added friction to remove any oil residue. Avoid touching the face (if possible) until you can wash. If you have baby wipes, give a quick wipe down of the area you think came into contact with the plant. (*See Appendix III: Avoiding Potential Dangers on the Hike.*)

- ***Know when to turn around.***
  This is crucial and should not be underestimated. There will be times when you and your child want different things, or when the weather or time of day doesn't seem to be cooperating with your plan. Resist the urge to keep going. The last thing you want is to be anxious or uncomfortable, so listen to your first instinct. As a parent, I fully believe that our instincts are heightened to keep our families safe and comfortable.

- ***Pre-plan your turnaround time and stick to it.***
  This will alleviate your stress and any decision-making later on.

Chapter 3

What Should I Pack?
Complete Pack, Snack, and First Aid Kit Checklists & Tips

As a new mom I got hit hard with baby brain, otherwise known as forgetfulness. I was always a list person, but packing lists became especially helpful. Lists are an amazing organizational tool; use them! I put my keys, phone, wallet—even my baby on that list!

If hiking is or becomes a habit for you, you will find that most of these things can stay in the backpack. But it's good to refer to the list from time to time so as not to forget the little things that can easily be overlooked. I've been out hiking, feeling proud of my preparedness, when I notice how dry and cracked my lips feel. I reach into my pocket and realize I forgot my chapstick, and I feel unsettled for the rest of the trip. As you get used to packing, you may just need a quick glance to make sure you are fully prepared.

Oh, and as a common law of leaving the house with little ones, always expect the *worst diaper situation you can imagine.* This way you will be sure to bring adequate clothing, wipes, diapers, and garbage baggies.

PACK LIST KEY
🌸Spring ☀️Summer 🍂Fall ❄️Winter
No symbol = pack in all seasons!

Infant Complete Pack List

- ❏ Four diapers
- ❏ Diaper changing pad/cloth
- ❏ Wipes
- ❏ Zip-lock bag for food waste, garbage, and dirty diapers
- ❏ Small toy with clip
- ❏ Bottle filled with water ☀️
- ❏ Bottle with milk/formula (if you are not breastfeeding)
- ❏ Infant snacks (*see "Snack Tip" below*)
- ❏ Spare infant clothes!
- ❏ Water and snacks for yourself for travel/trail (~24 oz. of water)
- ❏ Hats for you and child
- ❏ Compact First Aid Kit
- ❏ Map
- ❏ Sunscreen ☀️
- ❏ Lip balm ☀️ ❄️
- ❏ Organic insect repellent for exposed skin and insect repellent containing DEET for boots 🌸 ☀️ 🍂
- ❏ Sneakers or boots with traction and ankle support
- ❏ Baby carrier/backpack carrier
- ❏ Charged phone
- ❏ Wallet
- ❏ Keys

❏ Optional: Diaper changing pad/cloth
❏ Optional: binoculars
❏ Optional: pocket knife, headlamp, toilet paper
❏ Optional: water bladder (*see "Reduce Weight & Bulk Tip" below*)

Toddler Complete Pack List

❏ Four diapers or two extra undies
❏ Wipes
❏ Zip-lock bag for food waste, garbage, and dirty diapers
❏ Bottle or sippy cup with water
❏ Bottle with milk
❏ Snacks for child (*see "Snack Tip" below*)
❏ Retractable mirror to clip on if back carrying (also acts as a fun toy!)
❏ Water and snacks for yourself for travel/trail (~24 oz. of water)
❏ Hats for you and child
❏ Compact First Aid Kit
❏ Map
❏ Sunscreen ☀
❏ Lip balm ☀ ❄
❏ Organic insect repellent for exposed skin and insect repellent containing DEET for boots ❀ ☀ 🦟
❏ Sneakers or boots with traction and ankle support
❏ Baby carrier/backpack carrier
❏ Charged phone
❏ Wallet
❏ Keys

❏ Optional: diaper changing pad/cloth
❏ Optional: binoculars and/or toilet paper roll binoculars for child (they love them!)
❏ Optional: pocket knife, headlamp, toilet paper
❏ Optional: water bladder (*see "Reduce Weight & Bulk Tip" below*)

First Aid Kit Essentials

❏ Non-latex gloves
❏ Ziplock bag (storing the gloves in the bag is a handy way to ensure a bag for used gloves)
❏ Adhesive bandages (the sillier the better) of all sizes
❏ Gauze pads and medical tape
❏ Antiseptic towelettes
❏ Antibiotic ointment
❏ Sting-relief wipes
❏ EpiPen if known or potential serious allergic reaction to insect stings or bites
❏ Antihistamine (preferably liquid)
❏ Small packet of ibuprofen and/or acetaminophen tablets
❏ Tweezers
❏ Ice pack (optional)

 SNACK TIPS!

Once your child has begun to explore texture and tastes, try these great snacking foods! All three are great options for the trail or for anytime when you are on the go because they are:
- low spoilage risk
- belly fillers
- healthy
- low maintenance (in terms of mess and need for utensils)
- low bulk

Pancakes

Frozen homemade pancakes are a super on-the-go food and they fit just about anywhere. They are a great teething remedy if eaten when they are still frozen or cold. In a nutshell, they are lifesavers!

Avocados

Though avocados require a little extra foresight, they guarantee that your child will get a filling and nutritious meal. Be sure the avocado is ripe, and all you will need is a knife, spoon, and piece of foil to wrap up any leftovers. Cut it in half and spoon to feed!

Scrambled Eggs

Cut up the eggs and carry them in a small container. Your infant or toddler can feed themselves this delicious protein-packed snack. I also consider them a low choking hazard when you are on the move.

Don't forget yourself!

You will need extra energy, so be sure to bring trail mix with nuts, granola bars, or bananas to keep you going! Pack snacks that aren't bulky or difficult to eat on the move. Also avoid foods such as candy bars or chips. These foods are filled with empty calories and won't satisfy your mind and body for an extended period. Whatever you pack for yourself think **easy, filling and nutritious.**

 REDUCE WEIGHT & BULK TIP!

I've noticed that even when I have water, sometimes I don't drink enough. The little added hassle of stopping, unloading, and getting the water out of the pack can be just enough to deter me from drinking. In order to make hydration more convenient, I use a water bladder that easily fits into my backpack and my backpack carrier. Around 16 months old, my daughter figured out how to drink from it, too. My son was 11 months when he started using a water bladder and it kept him very entertained. If your child is able to drink from a straw, give it a try! This made packing water much easier and a lot less bulky. I knew the bladder would hold enough water for both me and my child, and we could both access the water without having to stop and unload.

Chapter 4

How Should I Carry My Child?
Carrying Methods, Stretches
for Self-Care & FAQ

There are many safe and appropriate ways to wear or carry your child on a hike. I recommend carrying your child the same way you would while out and about on daily routines. Do what is comfortable for both you and your child.

I first started hiking with my daughter when she was four months old. I front-carried her facing towards me until I felt she was ready to be in a backpack carrier. This is what worked for our family. However, I have hiked with women who have used various wraps, who have front-carried both facing in and facing out, who have back-carried, and who have had backpack carriers. These are all wonderful ways to engage with your child in nature. Again, the best way to carry your child on a hike is the way that will be most comfortable for both you and your child.

Before going out for a hike, it's a good idea to test your carrier closer to home. Be aware of how your body is feeling and where the weight is sitting. For your child, you will want to pay attention to how her hips are sitting, the position of her neck, and if any rubbing or redness appears around her thighs where her skin meets with the edge of a carrier. With the right carrying method, babies and younger toddlers will be at peace and even sleep during the hike. This in itself can be reason to celebrate! So it's well worth taking the time to ensure that both you and your child are comfortable with your carrier of choice. If your carrier doesn't feel quite right, don't hesitate to try a new one. There are many great options and tutorials out there to help you find the perfect fit.

Making Adjustments to the Carrier

As you hike, you'll want to make minor adjustments to the carrier to keep you and your little one comfortable. If a baby becomes fussy a breastfeeding mother may want to adjust the carrier so she can nurse, and having this flexibility in a carrier can be a game changer. When you're making adjustments, it's best if they can be done with ease. Frequent or complicated adjustments can be discouraging and frustrating for everyone, so having experience with your carrier can be very helpful. The following is a list of suggested adjustments that can be made to keep your body happy.

To relieve tension in your…

Shoulders—Shift weight onto your hips by loosening the shoulder strap and tightening waist strap. This works for both front and back-carry.

Waist—Add a sock under the strap for an extra cushion if you feel too much pressure on your waist or hip bone.

Hips—Loosen waist/hip strap and tighten shoulder straps. If you are back-carrying you can give the carrier a little boost while tightening the shoulder straps. This will raise your center of gravity to alleviate your hip area.

Back—Tighten your shoulder straps to bring your baby closer to you. Strain can build up by having too much slack in the shoulder straps or if your baby is moving around a lot. Your baby will either love or hate this adjustment. Give them a couple of minutes to get settled in the new position. Reducing the slack will also help your overall balance.

 COOL GEAR TIP FOR THE BACK CARRY!

With your precious cargo on your back, you will get curious about what they are up to or what condition they are in. Staying in tune is how we hike harmoniously with our little ones! Try a rearview mirror, also called a "babywearing rearview sling mirror." They are retractable and the perfect way to keep tabs on your baby's needs. They also double for a toy when your child needs a little extra entertainment.

Stretches for Self-Care

With each stage of carrying, from infant to toddler, you will notice the strain in different parts of your body. The following section provides stretches to help alleviate any soreness you may experience during or after the hike. Remember that self-care will make the overall experience more positive for both you and your child. Take the time to stretch before and after each hike to avoid tight or strained muscles. Be gentle with yourself both physically and mentally, and let your body guide your expectations and intentions for each outing. Some days you will naturally have more stamina for longer and more rigorous hikes. Other days you'll feel the greatest benefits from a more mellow and relaxed hike.

Front Carry

Lower Back

While you are hiking, tuck your tailbone under and engage your core. Rather than sticking your butt out, you can imagine that your tailbone is pointing to the ground and scooping slightly upward. This will protect your lower back. It feels funny at first, but it makes a big difference (especially for those with sensitive lower backs).

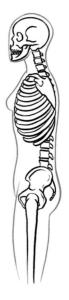

Chest

If your chest feels tight during a hike, expand your chest by imagining you are raising your heart to the sky. Push your shoulders back and try to touch your shoulder blades, and give your neck a gentle sway from side to side. After you are finished hiking, try a chest-opening exercise such as cat/cow, or repeat expanding your chest while trying to touch shoulder blades. This will open you up and alleviate any strain or stiffness you may have created in your chest.

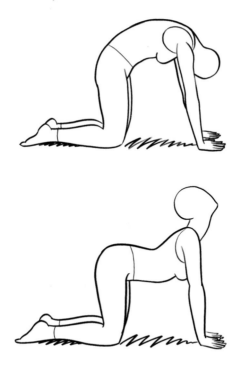

Back Carry & Backpack Carry

When back carrying, the bulk of the weight sits on your shoulders. You will notice that many of your adjustments will be to tighten the waist strap and loosen the shoulder straps to alleviate pressure on your upper back, shoulders, and neck. These adjustments will transfer the weight from your shoulders to your hips. Your waist straps should rest on your upper hip bone. You may find that the greater the weight, the tighter your waist straps will need to be. This can make your hips sore, so adding extra padding there with a sock or something soft can alleviate that pressure. During your breaks or after you are finished with your hike, you'll want to stretch and loosen your shoulders, neck, upper back, and hips.

Shoulders & Upper Back

Intertwine your arms in front of you, with one arm beneath the other. Try to lock your hands and keep your arms in a 90 degree position, bending at the elbow. Try to keep your shoulders back by picturing your shoulder blades touching. Take a deep breath and switch.

Neck
Gently roll your neck from side to side and all the way around. Look to the left and pause; look to the right and pause.

Hips
Stand with your legs spread and your hands on your hips. Feet face forward and knees are loose. Rotate your hips around clockwise a few times and then reverse.

Frequently Asked Carrier Questions

What carrier should I use?
Use a carrier that is comfortable for both you and your baby, sturdy, and easy to adjust. Any type of babywearing method that meets this criteria is appropriate.

How is a backpack carrier different from other carriers?
A backpack carrier differs from other carriers in that they have a frame and straps that are designed to distribute the baby's weight more comfortably over your body. Backpack carriers are an exciting step for children who are used to other carrying methods. For inward facing babies, this is the first time they can see what is coming and have a much wider field of view. For children used to the back-carry method, where they sit a bit lower on the back, the backpack carrier elevates them above your head. This allows them to see and experience much more.

When is my baby ready for a backpack carrier?

In order to use a backpack carrier, babies need to be able to sit up unassisted. I would recommend waiting until babies are at least 8 months old when they are a bit stronger and sturdier.

My child is getting too heavy for me in the backpack carrier but still likes to be carried. What can I do?

Backpack carriers come with a lot of storage room. This is great but can also add unnecessary weight. Try to lighten your load and carry only the essentials. Also try going back to a frameless carrier. Frameless carriers weigh less and are much easier to take your child in and out of, when they begin to walk on their own.

When should my child stop using a carrier?

Hikes naturally evolve into explorations once your child is fully walking on their own and you feel your child is ready to hike on their own. Shorten your walking distance to keep everyone positive and have a bag of tricks to keep them engaged. (*See Chapter 9: Hiking with the Independent Toddler*)

My child doesn't want to stay in the carrier. What can I do?

If your child isn't able to walk yet, they might be fussing due to hunger or sleepiness. You can try offering a snack or giving them a toy to play with (be sure to strap it on!). If they are learning how to walk or are an early walker, it might be a good time to let them try it out on their own!

Chapter 5

What Should I Wear?
Everything You Need to Know to Dress
for Success

When you're hiking with your baby or toddler, you will be carrying them for at least some of the hike, if not the entirety of it, depending on whether your toddler has started to express their need for independence. With this in mind, your clothing needs to be adaptable and layering your clothing is the best way to be flexible. Your level of comfort is very important. How you choose to dress will affect your endurance and mood on the hike. As you dress, be conscious of which layer will be the first to shed or add. This will help you plan, so you don't become trapped in your clothes under carrier straps.

Basic Layering Terminology

Base layer is the layer closest to your body. This layer should wick moisture away from your skin. In colder weather, your base should fit more snugly to keep heat closer to your body. In warmer weather, your base should fit more loosely to allow more air circulation.

Mid layer is the layer in between your base and your outermost clothing. In very cold weather, you may have two mid layers. This layer is the insulation layer, meaning that it traps your body heat.

Outer layer (or shell) is the layer exposed to the elements. This layer should be water repellent on rainy or snowy days, or windproof so that body heat is not lost to the wind (literally) when you want to maintain it. Since you will be generating more body heat when carrying a child, you may want an outer layer with zippers or flaps under the arms to easily release heat without making any major adjustments.

Materials Make A Difference

When you're on a hike your body heats or cools in response to your movement and its environment. You want to be wearing a fabric that is sensitive to these changes and helps your body maintain homeostasis. Understanding how different material responds to heat and moisture will help you dress for your hike, and remain comfortable throughout.

Cotton: Hot & Dry

Cotton is a great material when hiking in hot and dry weather. Cotton absorbs moisture, allowing it to sit close to your skin. As it dries it creates a cooling effect, which is wonderful in the summer, but can be dangerous in cool, windy, or cold weather. Most infant clothing is made of cotton—be aware that infants will cool down quickly when you take them out of the carrier. Changing yourself and your little one into dry clothing after a hike will reduce this effect (note: Denim is cotton).

Wool: Any Weather

Wool is extremely versatile because of its ability to wick moisture from your skin and help your body maintain a stable temperature. Wool will keep you warm even when wet, because it draws moisture away from your skin. Even in the summer, a wool sock can be very beneficial for sweaty feet, or if you are walking in wet areas. Another plus is that it is an antimicrobial, which means less odor! The downside is that it takes longer to dry than other materials and can be more costly.

Synthetic Blends: Cold, Humid, or Rainy

Common synthetic blends include fleece, polyester, polypropylene, nylon, or spandex. Like wool, they wick moisture away from your skin. This helps your body maintain a stable body temperature and keeps your body warm even when wet. Unlike wool, synthetic blends tend to dry quickly. These materials are especially great when hiking with your little one for areas that build up extra heat, such as where the carrier meets your body, and where your baby is making contact with your body. Synthetics can also be more affordable than wool options. Keep in mind that clothing doesn't have to be expensive in order to "work".

Dress for the Season, Layer by Layer

Below is an easy reference to dress for success in any hiking season. As you become more experienced, you can adapt this guide to better fit your personal preferences and needs. The lists are arranged from **base layer to outer layer.**

Spring & Fall Hiking

Feet: wool socks, boots or sneakers with good traction
Legs: synthetic leggings or pants
Upper body: wicking shirt, long-sleeved shirt with zipper or buttons that can easily be removed, vest
Hands: gloves (optional)
Head: hat or beanie to protect from sun/wind, sunglasses

Summer Hiking

Feet: wool socks, boots or sneakers with good traction
Legs: shorts or breathable lightweight pants
Upper body: wicking sleeveless shirt or loose t-shirt (cotton is okay but will stay damp under straps)
Head: hat to protect from sun, sunglasses

Winter Hiking

Feet: wool socks, boots or sneakers with good traction
Legs: nylon tights, long underwear (avoid cotton), pants
Upper body: snug-fitting undershirt made of wicking material, wool sweater or fleece, jacket or vest that opens or is made for front or back-carrying
Hands: gloves
Head: hat or beanie to protect from sun/wind, sunglasses

Rain/Snow Adjustments

Feet: gaiters for snow (optional)
Legs: rain pants over outer layer
Upper body: water-resistant outer shell
Hands: water-resistant gloves
Head: jacket with hood

Chapter 6

How Should I Dress My Child?

Intuitively, you may dress your child as you would dress yourself, and often this is a good rule of thumb (*see Chapter 5: What Should I Wear*). However, if you are babywearing, **the way you carry your child will influence the way you dress them**, and understanding this relationship will give you more confidence and peace of mind that your child is comfortable and safe and that you have dressed them to the best of your ability. Be sure to review "Materials Make a Difference" described in Chapter 5 and be practical when dressing your child. There are great clothing options for every budget, and knowing what fabrics to look for will help you choose what's best for yourself and your family. When your child is no longer in a carrier, you can use the same layering and fabric tips for them as you would for yourself.

Front Carrying in a Wrap

If you are front-carrying a baby who is almost fully covered in a wrap, dress her the same way you would if you were going for a walk outside. You and your baby will be sharing and trapping body heat. In cooler weather, you want to keep your baby as close as you can to your body to generate more heat. This will most likely be over your middle layer (or between your base and your mid layers, if your mid layer is a vest). In mild (spring or fall) weather, be aware of the fabric your child is wearing, especially if it's cotton, since she may lose body heat quickly once they are no longer in the carrier. Cotton isn't a wicking fabric, therefore any built up sweat will sit on her skin and make her feel cool. To maintain a comfortable body temperature, be sure to pack an extra pair of clothes for her for after the hike. In warmer weather, however, this will not be an issue and may even provide a much needed cool down. Below is a quick guide for dressing your child when front-carrying in a wrap.

Cold Weather: same clothing as "going for a walk," a beanie hat (fleece or wool), and an extra pair of clothes for after hike

Mild Weather: same clothing as "going for a walk," head protection from sun, and an extra pair of clothes for after hike

Warm Weather: same clothing as "going for a walk," and head protection from sun

Front Carrying with Head, Arms, and Legs Free

Since your child's extremities will be further away from your body heat, you should dress her in an additional layer. I do not recommend dressing your child in a jacket unless they will be worn over your outer layer, or if your outer layer will be left open, because of the risk of your child over-heating. This is especially the case if you have a special babywearing jacket that is designed to keep your front carrier (or back carrier) completely covered. In general, the further your child is from your own body heat, the less heat she will have. In the winter, this means more layers for children. In the summer, this may mean fewer layers for them. If your child likes to get down and explore on her own, dress her in shoes that have good traction and that she can easily walk in (not those shoes two sizes too big that we are all guilty of letting them wear!) Below is a quick guide for dressing your child when front-carrying with your child's head, arms, and legs free.

Cold Weather: base layer, mid layer, jacket (only if worn over your outer layer), socks, shoes, a beanie hat (fleece or wool), and an extra pair of clothes for after hike

Mild Weather: same clothing as "going for a walk," head protection from sun, and an extra pair of clothes for after hike

Warm Weather: same clothing as "going for a walk," and head protection from sun

Backpack and Back Carrying

For this section, we'll assume that you're wearing your child on top of your outer-most layer, and therefore she is not sharing your body heat. In this case, we need to consider the effects of sun, cold and wind, and plan accordingly. You will want to use the layering system and pay particular attention to your child's head. Some backpacks are equipped with sun-shades, while others are not. In cooler weather, dress your child in a hat that she is likely to leave on. A rearview retractable mirror will be helpful here, so that you can easily check on her. Also make sure that your child isn't getting too much wind in her face—teary eyes can be a good indicator. As you spend more time with your child outdoors, your confidence in your judgment will grow. Below is a quick guide for dressing your child when you carry them on your back.

Cold Weather: base layer, mid layer, windproof and water resistant jacket or snowsuit, wool socks, shoes, and a hat or beanie that will stay on your child's head (fleece or wool)

Mild Weather: long-sleeved shirt, vest or lightweight jacket, long pants that cover ankles, socks, shoes, hat that protects from sun or beanie (fleece or wool)

Warm Weather: t-shirt or long-sleeved lightweight shirt, lightweight pants or shorts, socks (optional), shoes/sandals, and head protection from sun

 COLD WEATHER TIP!

Nylon stockings make an excellent base layer for your child. They are easy to find in most children's stores and inexpensive! Nylon is a wicking fabric that draws moisture away from the skin, allowing the body to maintain a comfortable temperature. Stockings fit snuggly, keeping warmth closest to the body while also making it easy to layer without making your little one too bulky.

Part Three

Taking Ownership of Your Experiences in Nature

Chapter 7

Creating Positive and Nurturing Experiences in Nature

Establishing Your Foundation: Preparedness + Intention

Your ability to create positive and nurturing outdoor experiences with your child will come with much more ease once you have established your foundation. A strong foundation built through *preparedness* will allow you the mental space to be present with your child on the hike. The checklists and information in the previous chapters are designed to prepare you, so that once you are on the hike you won't be worrying about whether you packed the extra wipes, brought the right snacks, or whether your baby is dressed appropriately. You will know you came prepared and will be ready for your adventure.

I like to refer to your nature outing with your child as an "adventure," because it is! One of the best things you can do to keep your hike exciting, and not disappointing, is to avoid "setting yourself up." There were times when I would get back from a hike feeling disappointed because it hadn't gone the way I'd planned. It's easy to feel this way, which is why I suggest setting an *intention*—rather than a plan—for your hike before you set out together.

An intention gives you a focus for what you hope to achieve, without being as restrictive as a "plan." It can be vague or specific, but try to keep it simple. Your intention could be something like, "today I feel great, and I am ready for a work-out." When you come back to your intention on the hike, it will motivate you to move a little faster. Another example might be, "today I'm going to take this time to stroll through the woods and catch up with a friend." This shifts the focus from the hike itself and reminds you that what's important is to have some much-needed time with your friend. You may choose to set an intention to be able to learn and identify one new plant. Whatever the case, be realistic about what you expect from both yourself *and* your child while on your hike.

When setting your intention, be mindful of how your child is feeling and acting. Some days I felt discouraged, and found that my intention was based solely on what I wanted to achieve and wasn't really taking into account my daughter's needs on that day. Yes, I really wanted to see the scenic viewpoint, but I had to turn around because my daughter wasn't feeling it. And while feeling down is totally okay when something doesn't go the way you want, it does serve as a reminder to practice being more flexible. If I feel discour-aged, I remind myself that my goal is to have a positive experience with my daughter, so that we will both value our time in nature. Check in with your child, and set your intention based on both of your moods. As I mentioned before, remember that your intention is more like a guide, and not meant to restrict you.

Mindfulness and Flexibility

When you are *mindful* on your hike, you are in tune with yourself, your child, and your surroundings. As stated before, you will run into the unexpected, and how you deal with this will dictate the overall experience. Going into a hike with a sense of adventure and realistic expectations will allow you to better adapt to different situations as they arise. Did the explosive diaper ruin your trip? Or were you able to laugh it off, clean it up and move on? Your ability to be *flexible* is essential in creating a nurturing experience with your child. Flexibility means that you are adapting to the needs of your situation and environment. If hiking with your child becomes a habit, flexibility will become one of your most prized skills.

When my daughter was about ten months old, my husband and I made the switch to a backpack carrier. In order to use a backpack carrier your baby must be able to sit up unassisted, which usually means that a child in a backpack carrier is a larger child. When my daughter reached about two years old, I finally had to admit to myself that I couldn't carry her as long as I used to be able to. Rather than a three hour hike, I was finding I could only last up to an hour or so. No matter how much I adjusted my straps, I found that my posture was becoming hunched—I was sore, and I was bummed. Up until this point, my hikes were my workout and my reset button. I had grown stronger and my daughter and I were sharing real intimate benefits of being in nature—the fresh air, the silence, the escape. It was perfect! But it was clear now that something had to change. I had to be more realistic about what I wanted versus what I could expect from a hike, and also adapt to a whole new way of experiencing nature with my growing child. Now that I couldn't carry her as long, she would have to begin to hike on her own. And this meant slowing down and accepting that our hikes wouldn't be my exercise anymore. It also meant that I would have to learn new ways to nurture our time together, and new ways to engage her wonder and curiosity about the natural world.

The need for adjustment and flexibility was a good lesson to accept. As parents we will always have to shift and adjust to the growth of our children both physically *and* emotionally, and this was just one tiny example. It was an opportunity to reflect about my intention of spending time outdoors with my child. For me this meant lowering my physical expectations and making the hikes more about my daughter rather than myself. Ultimately, being more flexible allowed me the space to take the hike slower, go a shorter distance, and experience more of my surroundings. It enabled me to bring my daughter into that space, and for the first time, see the forest as she saw it.

Practice of Presence & Awareness
Many of us choose to make time to be outside in nature to escape the mundane—our daily routines or the air we are used to breathing. It's about tak-

ing time for ourselves and our families. Going on a hike in the woods or a walk in the park means time away from everyday chatter, time for healing, time for building relationships, and time for creating positive experiences together.

Surprisingly, it takes practice to leave everything behind. Being present in our experience helps us stay calm, allows us to savor the time with our little ones, and makes us a safer and more aware hiker. I've included the following list to help open your awareness while on the trail. As your child grows, you can use these open-ended questions to stay in tune with each other and share your observations. It will also help build their confidence and sense of ownership in their experience.

- *What colors do you see?*
- *Do all the trees look the same?*
- *Look closer...how many different shaped leaves can you find?*
- *Do you see any patterns on the bark?*
- *Is the bark rough or smooth?*
- *Is the trail wide or narrow?*
- *Can you see any trail markers on the trees? What color are they?*
- *What do you hear?*
- *Are there noises from cars? Are you close to a road?*
- *Can you hear insects or animals? What kind do you think live in this habitat?*
- *Can you see or hear water? Is it moving or still?*
- *How does the air feel on your skin?*

Chapter 8

Encouraging Lasting Memories

Sometimes I catch myself in the middle of an amazing moment with my children and I think to myself, "I really hope they can remember this when they're older." Actually I hope the same for *myself.* As a new mom I would often think, "I will never forget this moment." And now with my second child I realize how much I did, in fact, forget amidst the chaos of daily life! With our busy routines and ever-growing pressure to provide a smorgasbord of opportunity for our children, it's easy to treat our activities like a checklist—once they are over, we move on to the next one without too much reflection. But time in nature has repeatedly been shown to make people feel less stressed, more happy and whole. So let's dwell here for a moment and explore ways in which we can be mindful in protecting and enhancing the special experiences we're sharing with our children in nature. I like to think that the experiences we share with our babies become ingrained or stored inside of them. And that perhaps by creating lasting memories, specifically in nature, our babies will grow into adults who inherently feel a connection with nature and an urgency to preserve and protect it.

Keep it Positive

Preparation and mindfulness are so important when you begin to hike with your family. By placing a value on these these processes, you are intentionally creating room for a more positive experience. It's like a trickle-down effect. When you know you have prepared, your mind is less worried, more at ease, and able to be present—your baby will pick up on this. Babies are so quick to learn what brings them comfort (and what doesn't) and you want your time in nature to be a comforting experience. If you repeatedly create comforting hiking experiences with your baby, they'll learn that being in nature is a good feeling. When your baby has found this happy place, they may even take a restful nap. While neither of my children are particularly good nappers, I eventually learned that both would fall asleep when we were out for a babywearing hike. Through a collection of experiences, they learned that the woods were a safe and comfortable place. A baby who is calm and at peace is already demonstrating her sense of ownership in the experience.

Toddlers will demonstrate a more dramatic sense of ownership. They will seem more fearless as they leave your side to explore. Their newly found freedom and empowerment are no doubt a positive experience for them, but remember that it's up to you to set boundaries that are both comfortable for you and safe, in order to keep the experience positive for everyone (*see Appendix III: Avoiding Potential Dangers on a Hike*). You can help a toddler take ownership of their experiences by returning to the same place or visiting the same trails. This allows them to gain familiarity with an area and will build their confidence in navigating. My daughter enjoys our hikes, but her favorites are the ones she is most familiar with, and gets to lead the way.

Using Our Senses

Engaging our senses while on a hike is another way we can excite our memory. Think back to a smell or sound that you have heard as an adult, and how quickly it brought you back to a particular place in time. Children especially are sensory oriented, which is why making a point to touch, smell, listen, or point out something you see can be so exciting and memorable. The forest is filled with fun textures to touch: tree bark, leaves, moss, and dirt. Babies will even try to mimic you when you smell a flower. You can also practice using your senses with your child by having conversations about what she is seeing, hearing, smelling, or feeling. Even if your child isn't verbal yet, she is learning from your example. You can find prompt questions at the end of Chapter 7 to get you started.

Reflecting Together

Reflecting together with our children about our experiences also helps us strengthen our memory and lets your child know that the experience was meaningful and worthwhile. Usually on our way home, I'll pick one or two things to talk about that happened along the hike. I also let my children know how special it was for me to be with them and how excited I am to do it again. By revisiting things we saw, heard or did along the way, we are reinforcing our positive experience together. And each time we revisit it, it makes that memory stronger and more likely to create a lasting impression.

Pictures are another easy tool for encouraging lasting memories. It's amazing and amazingly fun to hear the details that children can recollect when given a visual clue! Whether you and your child are scrolling through pictures together on your phone or flipping through a photo album, having a visual representation will go a long way.

For young explorers, it seems almost intuitive to collect natural mementos or "tokens of appreciation." Almost immediately, my daughter started to stuff her pockets with rocks and acorns as soon as she was able to hike on her own. And while this provided a great opportunity to talk about shape, size, color, seasons, and even food chains, I did have to grapple with the Leave No Trace principle #4—leave what you find. Ultimately as parents, it's our responsibility to teach our children how to be good stewards of our environment, and each one of us will have to draw that line. With that said, a humble collection box can become a source of pride and something you and your child can come back to again and again.

Nature Centered Activities

Using nature or natural items as the foundation for an activity is a wonderful way to keep a child engaged with the *concept* of nature. These simple, yet carefully crafted activities allow children to take a concept and create something tangible. Nature-centered activities are meaningful because they invite children to apply their creative expression to explore nature in their own authentic way. There is no limit to what can be considered a nature-centered activity and can be based in art, science, culture, history, math, geography, you name it! Whichever style of activity you choose to explore with your child, be sure to let them lead the way. Allow it to be about their experience rather than the one you want them to have. I say this, because I've fallen into my own trap, where I've had an idea of how I wanted something to go, and quickly lost my daughter's attention because it differed too much from her own vision. I assure you it will be much more memorable for them if you allow them that freedom. The following are suggestions for nature-centered activities:

- *Construct a hand-made nature journal*
- *Create a collage, drawing, or painting*
- *Design a walking stick*
- *Put together a photo album of natural "discoveries"*
- *Build a nest from natural materials*
- *Paint eggshells*
- *Start a collection box*
- *Observe a plant in your yard to see how it changes through the seasons*
- *Go for a nature scavenger hunt*

Chapter 9

Hiking with the Independent Toddler

The Steady Walker

There will come a time when your little one will be ready to start exploring more independently. It won't happen all at once, but you can expect it sometime between when she becomes a steady walker and when she gets too heavy for you to carry the entire time. At this stage, children are also becoming better communicators and beginning to enjoy the new feeling of independence that comes with learning how to walk. When you see your child's look of wonderment as she begins to explore her surroundings, a real sense of joy bubbles up within you. It is an amazing feeling.

This newfound independence marks a new phase for both you and your child's time in nature. You can expect a lot of ups and downs—literally, as your child transitions from the carrier, to walking, back to the carrier, and so on. For our family, this change began a few months before my daughter turned two. Up until this point she had been happy exploring her world from the backpack, telling us what she saw and heard along the way. She was focusing on her communication skills, and now seemed to be ready for more. Coincidentally, I was finding that my body needed more frequent breaks from her weight. So the timing seemed appropriate—for me, physically, and for my daughter, developmentally—to start hiking on her own. Like many children, her explorations started from the ground up. She loved picking up things like rocks, acorns, gravel and leaves, and collecting them in her pockets.

The Tension of Independence

Even as this great need for independence begins to set in, your child still feels the need to be close to you. At this stage, our poor little ones are tormented with their internal emotions. And what this means for hiking with an independent toddler is that we can't expect them to walk for the entire time just yet. Even if they are physically capable of walking, they may still emotionally want to be carried. When my daughter reached this point, I brought along an Ergobaby carrier to back-carry her when she needed it. The Ergo was more lightweight than a backpack carrier and was more compact to tote when she was walking. I also found ways to increase her engagement with her environment so that she would be willing to walk for longer periods of time.

Let Them Lead the Way

As your little one grows, you will need to constantly be thinking of ways to engage your child while on the hike. Children are naturally curious and want to have fun, and they also like to feel a sense of control—so follow their lead. Your role here will take on a whole new dimension, as you become more of a facilitator whose job is to foster positive experiences while also setting safe boundaries. This can be a time of uncertainty and will require a "bag of tricks," but I promise you will surprise yourself with what you can come up with on the spot. And the payoff is well worth this new challenge. Your children will feel a greater sense of control, develop confidence, and become empowered by their experiences in the outdoors. With your guidance and persistence, they will develop a deeper connection with natural spaces.

Bag of Tricks

Increase your child's engagement in nature with these activities:

Look for animal tracks in the snow or mud.
- What animal is it?
- How fast do you think they were moving?
- Which direction were they heading?
- How was the animal feeling?

Touch different textures.
- Smooth vs. bumpy bark
- Velvety leaves vs. papery leaves
- Moss (nature's carpet)

Look for trail markers (blazes).
- What color trail are we on?
- Which way is it telling us to go?

Give incentives.
- A post-hike chocolate milk was a biggie for us.

• Use caution and be mindful of the incentives you choose!

Create obtainable challenges.
• Look for an object (a letter Y stick on the ground).
• Find rock or root climbing challenges (scrambles).

Choose a hike where you know animals will be.
• Turtle ponds
• Places with frogs or tadpoles
• Don't underestimate chipmunks and squirrels!

Choose a hike with fun features.
• Bridges
•Water to cross
• Rocks to climb
• Logs to explore

Sing a song.
• Make up your own
• Use a familiar tune and change the words
Tune of "We're Following the Leader"
"We're going on a hikey, a hikey, a hikey,
We're going on a hikey, to see what we can find…"

Visit the same place.
• This gives your child a chance to become familiar with a place.
• Your child develops sense of control because they know what to expect.

- Your child can lead the way.
- Pick a place where your child can walk almost the entire distance.

Find muddy puddles!

- Rain boots and rain pants recommended (for you too!)

Bring a favorite toy to share the adventure.

- One that won't be ruined when you wash it.

Let go (a little) and have fun!

Chapter 10

Basic Map Reading

Most of the places you'll decide to hike will have some sort of map showing trails and a layout of the general surrounding area. It's a good idea to get a printed map, and to have an idea of where you would like to go on that map *before* you head out. You can download map apps and pictures to your phone, but I still find it best to rely on recent and printed maps, just in case cell phone service is disrupted or your phone battery dies. If you find printed maps intimidating, or if you'd like to brush up on your map reading skills, then this chapter is for you. And remember—just because you have a map, doesn't mean you can't get lost!

This chapter walks you through the common features found on most maps. If your map does not include the basic features we cover, I suggest finding another map. As you read through this section, it will be helpful to have a map in hand, preferably one that covers a location you are familiar with so that you have a better sense of how all the features fit together throughout the landscape.

Scale

Every map should include some sort of scale to help you calculate or estimate the distance you are traveling. Usually you can find the scale in the key (or legend), but sometimes it will be elsewhere. If your map doesn't have a scale, consider ditching it. Once you have chosen a trail that you would like to hike, the best way to determine the distance is by tracing the trail with a piece of string and comparing it to the scale on the map. Twists and turns in a trail can really add distance, and using the string helps account for distance that may otherwise be overlooked. If you do not have a string, do your best to account for any switchbacks in the trail.

Once you have the distance, you can begin to estimate the amount of time you will need to allocate for this hike. My general rule of thumb is that, at a slow to moderate pace, you will hike approximately ***one mile every 30 minutes.*** This may vary depending on the inclines and amount of weight you are carrying. To be on the safe side, and to allow for frequent and unexpected stops, always overestimate the amount of time you think it will take.

Understanding the scale of a map will also help when you want to be spontaneous and try a new trail in the middle of a hike. Say you find yourself at a fork in the trail and you're curious about taking the left trail rather than the right one you usually take. When you have an understanding of the scale, you can refer to it and calculate if you and your child are up to hiking the distance the uncharted trail may require. This is when the safety tips outlined in Chapter 2 play a major role. Always plan a turnaround time, and stick to it.

Trail Markers

Trail markers, commonly called **blazes,** are used to mark trails so that you can follow a particular trail and not get lost. They often appear as painted lines on trees and rocks or color plates nailed to a tree. Usually they can be seen from either direction you are traveling along the trail. Your map may show trails using different colors, symbols, or patterns. When trails begin, end, or intersect with other trails, you will see some sort of symbol helping you stay on the right track. Take a minute to familiarize yourself with these symbols in case your map does not include this feature.

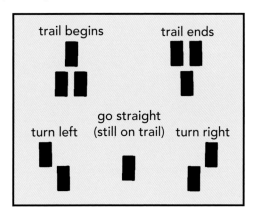

Elevation

Topographic maps use contour lines to represent changes in elevation. Some of the lines will be marked with numbers showing how many feet above sea level that point is. Contour lines are evenly spaced. The space between contour lines is called the elevation contour interval. The legend on the map will label the interval. For example, if the elevation contour interval is 20 feet, the space between each line shows either a decrease or increase of twenty feet. The closer the lines are together, the steeper the descent or ascent will be. Contour lines that are more spread out, means a flatter topography.

Interpreting the Map

Interpreting a map can be an enjoyable challenge. As you practice, you will notice that your ability to visualize a trail will strengthen. You can begin to interpret a map by locating a trail on the map. Use the map legend or key and select a feature that interests you, like a scenic view. Find the starting point (i.e. a parking area) and use your finger to trace the trail(s) that will lead you to your point of interest. Keeping in mind scale, changes in elevation, and land features, start to envision what you will see along the way. *How far should you walk before the trail bends to the right? Is the elevation contour interval showing a steep change in elevation, or will this trail be suitable for your toddler to walk? Will you be able to safely carry your infant up to the scenic view if there is a steep climb? If you find yourself walking for longer than you expected and you haven't seen a trail blaze in a while, are there land features such as water or roads that you should expect to hear or see?* This practice will give you greater flexibility in choosing new trails to hike, it will build confidence in your navigational skills, and it will help you prepare, assess, and manage potential risks. Map interpretation is also a rewarding practice to share with an older child as their skills and confidence develop in the outdoors.

Understanding North

If you are practicing using a compass with your map, it's important to understand map orientation and the difference between magnetic north and true north. All maps will reference north in one way or another, whether it be through a compass rose or longitudinal gridlines. Your compass will point to magnetic north (MN) due to the earth's magnetic field. True north (TN) refers to the North Pole, which is the axis of the earth's rotation. Magnetic north and true north do not refer to the same point. In fact, due to shifts in the earth's structure (i.e. plate tectonics) the location of MN changes every year. Consider this when using older maps. Depending on the map you are using, the shifting of MN over time could explain why your compass might not align with the directional north indicated by your map. Large metal objects can also interfere with your compass's ability to get a good read. Some maps include blue UTM (Universal Transverse Mercator) gridlines, which point to true north. These maps usually include magnetic declination, which shows how many degrees your compass will differ from true north. Cell phone compasses use magnetometers which means they point to MN but are capable of showing TN as well. In general, just having a basic idea of where north is will be enough to ensure a successful hike with your child

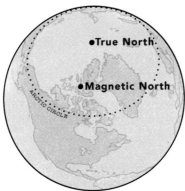

True North vs Magnetic North

Magnetic North migration

Appendices

A Note About the Appendices

The following appendices are regional resources for hiking in the NYC Metropolitan area. Some of the information may be useful outside of this area, but flora and fauna will vary state to state.

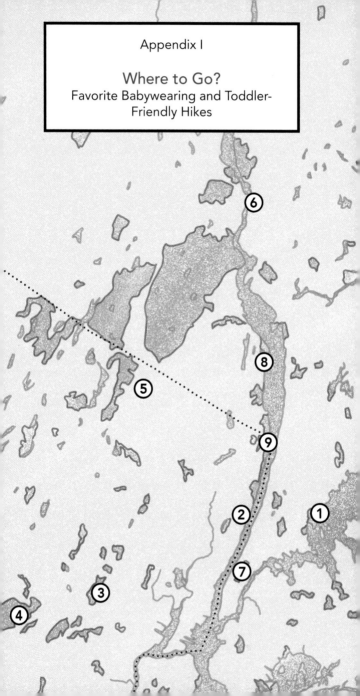

Appendix I

Where to Go?
Favorite Babywearing and Toddler-
Friendly Hikes

1. Kazimiroff Trail, Pelham Bay, N.Y.

Pelham Bay is located in the Bronx. It is New York City's largest park. The Kazimiroff Trail is an absolute gem and an important stop over for migratory birds. You must visit this natural space! The New York-New Jersey Trail Conference calls it a "natural mosaic of forest meadow and salt marsh." Despite the frequent air traffic, this trail takes you out of the city and makes you feel like you are surrounded by wilderness. Follow the blue trail numbered 1-12 and 16-18 (numbers 13-15 are part of the red trail). You will dabble in and out of woodlands and view panoramas of salt-tolerant grasses looking over the Long Island Sound. The northern section of the trail links to a wooden boardwalk through a marsh, leading you to a small island overlooking a coastal panoramic that resembles the Mediterranean. There are many small unmarked trails, so unless you have planned for exploration time, it may be best to stick to the marked trails.

Distance: ~ 2 miles
Duration: ~ 2 hours, including viewing stops
Intensity: easy
Accessibility: public transportation and car
Free PDF map available online at www.nycgov-parks.org by searching "PDF Kazimiroff Nature Trail."

2. Flat Rock Brook, Englewood, N.J.

This is a wonderful forest where you can practice babywearing hiking or have your toddler hike alongside you. The trails are relatively flat, with the exception of a few minor ups and downs. Many trails connect to each other, which makes it easy to shorten or lengthen any route that you have chosen. The various habitats within this relatively small area make for abundant wildlife sighting opportunities! You are sure to see something that will get you and your little one excited about your adventure in nature. If you visit in the spring and early summer you may get to see tadpoles in the Quarry Pond near the Nature Center Building. In addition to deer, chipmunks, and an abundance of birds, there is a family of snapping turtles that swim below the Mystery Bridge. The bridge sits beside a large flat rock that provides a perfect place to break and eat a snack.

For a longer loop, leave the parking lot and head northeast on the white loop trail. Continue along the red trail until the Mystery Bridge. If you are using the NYNJTC map, you will recognize the bridge by the flat rock overlooking a wetland area. This route will loop back to the rock after ~15-20 minutes of walking. Cross the bridge and you will continue on the green loop trail, until it meets with the yellow trail. Make a left to take the yellow loop trail around a small loop until it brings you back to the green trail (or you can skip the yellow all together for a shorter hike). Once you are back to where the yellow and green meet, follow the green trail back to the Mystery Bridge for a rest. From here, continue up the red trail heading east. The trail will continue south back towards the parking area. From the red trail, take the blue loop trail heading southwest until you meet with the purple and white loop trails. You can take either the purple or white loop trail back to the parking area. If you follow the purple trail, you will need to make a right onto the white trail to get back to Quarry Pond (the parking area). Note: Restrooms are only available when the Nature Center is open. You may want to call ahead.

Distance: ~2 miles
Duration: 1 to 1.5 hours
Intensity: easy
Accessibility: car
Free maps available at white loop trailhead across from Nature Center. Maps also available through NYNJ Trail Conference: Hudson Palisades Trails #108.

3. South Mountain Reservation, N.J.
If you are on the hunt for a good waterfall hike to do with your little ones, check out Hemlock Falls in the South Mountain Reservation. This hike and waterfall area will not disappoint. It's great fun for kids and dogs who like to splash in the pools beneath the falls. If you are babywearing, be aware of loose rocks and tricky footing in some areas.

While there are many ways to access Hemlock Falls, the most straightforward way is to enter South Mountain Reservation on Crest Drive off of South Orange Avenue (you will see a small parking area at the entrance). Walk down the "Openwood Trail" (a wide trail that runs adjacent to South Orange Ave.) for about 15 to 30 minutes, depending on your pace. The trail will lead you to a large descending staircase. At the end, turn right and continue on the yellow trail (Lenape Trail) until you hit the falls. To add exploration for sturdy toddlers, you can take the staircase adjacent to the falls marked by a red blaze (or bullseye). This will take you above the falls where you can explore and splash around in small pools. Be sure to bring an extra pair of shoes and socks for your toddler!

Distance: 1.5 to 2 miles
Duration: 1 to 2 hours
Intensity: easy to moderate
Accessibility: car
Maps available through South Mountain Conservancy www.somocon.org.

4. Great Swamp National Wildlife Refuge, N.J.

For babywearers interested in birding and for families with younger children and toddlers, I highly recommend the small boardwalk trail off of the Wildlife Observation Center. It's short enough where your little one can walk while also offering a lot to observe and take in. The information kiosk has a colorful and informative display of the wildlife that lives in the area. The entire trail is on a boardwalk and ends with a blind, a small semi-closed structure where you can observe birds though small windows. My two-year-old loved this part! Remember that you are in a swamp, so prepare yourself with the proper bug repellent. You can pick up a map at the Wildlife Observation Center, which will show you all the viewing areas, parking, and a few other trails in the eastern section of the refuge. Restrooms are available at the Center.

Distance: 2 miles
Duration: 1 hour
Intensity: easy
Accessibility: car
Free maps available at the Wildlife Observation Center.

5. Ramapo Valley County Reservation, N.J.

Ramapo is a place that needs to be explored time and time again. It's a place I hope you make a point to visit and revisit. This particular hike is not recommended for toddlers, though there is a pond near the parking lot that is perfect for toddlers and dog walkers. This is a highly trafficked area, but once you get to the more remote trails you will feel a sense of solitude (with the comfort of cell reception). This is one of my favorite hikes because it makes me feel like I am doing a real hike (like the ones we did before parenthood!) and it is truly an amazing hike for babywearers. Please be aware that there are active bear in the area. Be sure to make your presence known by clapping your hands, blowing a whistle, or talking loudly (*see Appendix III: Avoiding Potential Dangers on the Hike*). On a clear day, your effort will pay off with breathtaking views of New York City and a beautiful reservoir where you can rest and take in the scenery. And if it has recently rained a lot, this trail will even provide an amazing view of a waterfall. (*Note: the reservoir area gets very busy on the weekends*)

My favorite loop starts just off of Route 202, south of Darlington Ave. Leave the parking area and follow the yellow trail. Pass over a bridge and follow the large trail with the pond on your right. Continue until you reach a tree that marks the beginning of the blue trail. Make a right to follow the yellow trail and keep the pond on your right-side. You will then come to a tree on the left, that marks the beginning of the silver trail. Make a left here, over a small wooden bridge, to follow the yellow trail and begin a strenuous climb. The yellow trail will eventually meet up with the blue trail. If you are feeling tired, you can shorten this hike by taking the blue trail down when the yellow trail splits to the right. You can follow the yellow trail here for a few steps to see the views of NYC and then backtrack for the quick route down (blue trail) or continue along the yellow trail to reach the reservoir. When you get to the reservoir the path is a little tricky to follow. At the top of the large rock overlooking the reservoir, turn to the left and you will see that the yellow trail meets up with the pink. Follow the yellow trail with the water to your left. After the reservoir, you will start on your way down. Just before a stone bridge you will make a right, off the main path, to follow the yellow trail past the waterfall. You are almost there! The loop will return you to the main path where you began. Turn right onto the yellow trail to return to the parking area.

Distance: ~3.8 miles
Duration: 2 to 3 hours
Intensity: strenuous

Accessibility: car
Maps available through NYNJ Trail Conference: North Jersey Trails #115.

6. Garrison, N.Y.

This location is perfect for babywearing parents who want a bit of a workout and easy and convenient access from New York City. The Metro North train will have you there in around one hour. Don't miss the shaded gazebo if you plan to stop for a break to change diapers, eat a snack, or take in the views of the Hudson River. This trail is loaded with rich history worth reading about on the kiosks located near the pond at the southeastern portion of the trail. Along the way, you will see river views, deciduous forests (that are stunning in the fall), streams and ponds, and a variety of birds and other wildlife.

From the Garrison train platform, head to the southwest section of the parking area to find the trailhead. Following the blue trail, you will see a bridge on your right passing over the train tracks. If you want a shorter hike, cross over the tracks to Arden Point. This section of Garrison offers an easier hike and beautiful views of the Hudson River. The shorter distance and easier terrain here, are a great fit for hiking with toddlers. Otherwise, to stay on the main trail, continue on the blue until you get to the white trail, called the Glenclyffe Loop. This will lead you to the gazebo (up the stone stairs on your right) and onto the red trail. The trail will open into a large field overlooking the Hudson River, The large building behind this area belongs to the Open Space Institute. This is a great place to play and let those little legs free to run or wobble. Near the bench overlooking the river you can pick up the red trail if you have lost sight of it. Follow the red trail down into the valley, pass the pond, and through the bamboo thickets. Eventually you will go up an incline that leads you to a field. You'll have to walk along the road before cutting back in on the left, following the white (Glenclyffe Loop). This will bring you back towards the gazebo. From here, follow the same way you took in. From the gazebo it should take about 15 minutes to get back to the parking area. If you maintain a moderate pace, you will get a little workout, and have time for a short break before catching your train. (Note: this trail can be a little tricky to follow, so be sure to bring your map)

Distance: ~2.5 miles
Duration: 1.5 to 2 hours
Intensity: moderate
Accessibility: public transportation and car
Maps available through NYNJ Trail Conference: East Hudson Trails #101.

7. Central Park Brambles, New York City

Whether you live in New York City or not, a trip to the Brambles is worth it for any bird enthusiast. At any time of year, you're likely to run into a knowledgeable birder or nature photographer who will be glad to share a cool find. It's also the perfect place to see happy city people and tourists alike appreciating the city's natural resources and green space. Most of the paths are stroller friendly, but a free-roaming toddler may prove advantageous for getting into the nooks and crannies that make this Olmsted park so unique. The trails can easily trick your sense of direction, but looking for landmarks and buildings will keep you on your "NSEW" (north, south, east, and west).

Distance: ~2 miles
Duration: ~1 hour
Intensity: easy
Accessibility: public transportation and car
Free maps are available at info kiosks near entrances of Central Park.

8. Hook Mountain, N.Y.

For those looking for a more challenging baby-wearing hike, Hook Mountain is your go-to. It's challenging but brief inclines keep you feeling strong, the level trails keep you engaged, and breathtaking views of the Hudson River make it all worth it. Enter the trail through Rockland Lake State Park. Continue ahead on the main park road, which curves to the right, and proceed for 1.4 miles to a three-way intersection. Here, the main road bears left, but you should continue ahead onto Landing Road (marked by a "No Outlet" sign). After passing a fire station on the right, park in the spaces provided on the right side of the road, just before the barricade blocking the road. Follow the aqua trail the whole way. There will be three scenic views. Your final view (and turnaround point) is a large, exposed rock with views of the Hudson River and Tappan Zee

Bridge, officially named the Governor Mario M. Cuomo Bridge. This is a perfect place to take it all in and have a snack or lunch. If you visit during spring or fall migration you'll likely see birders participating in bird count surveys. For an even more enriching experience, ask them what they see! (Note: If your toddler is walking and being carried, allow more time, and be prepared to carry their weight up some hills)

Distance: ~4 miles
Duration: 2.5 to 3 hours
Intensity: moderate to strenuous
Accessibility: car
Maps available through NYNJ Trail Conference: Hudson Palisades Trails #110.

9. Palisades State Line Lookout, N.J./N.Y.

This location seems to have it all: family-friendly hikes, views of the Hudson River, a snack and gift shop, and a bathroom. There are a few different hikes that you can take that vary in length and intensity. For a nice, short hike, leave the parking lot from the northwest section and follow the F trail heading west. Follow signs and take a right onto the C trail. After crossing over old Route 9W, follow the E trail. At the fork, you can turn left onto the aqua trail to a scenic view, or make a right to continue on the E trail, which will take you back to the State Line Lookout and parking lot. This trail is perfect for toddlers and babywearing because it is relatively flat. It also gives you the option to add distance or head to some scenic views. (Note: the hike to the scenic view near the cliff is very steep. Use caution.)

Distance: ~2 miles
Duration: ~1 hour
Intensity: easy
Accessibility: car
*Maps available through NYNJ Trail Conference:
Hudson Palisades Trails # 109.*

Field Identification Guide
PLANTS & TREES

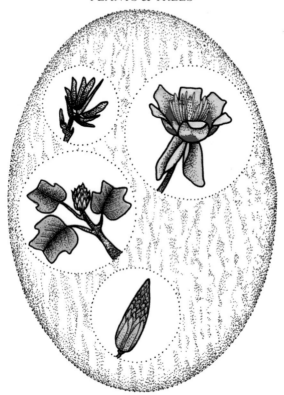

Tulip Tree
Liriodendron tulipifera

The Tulip Tree, also known as Yellow Poplar, is a beautiful tree that stands tall and straight in the deciduous forest. Mature trees have a diamond-like pattern on their bark. The best time to look for this tree is in the spring when it's flowers are in full bloom—one of the showiest flowers in the spring forest! Tulip tree seeds are eaten by squirrels and birds.

Poison Ivy ☠
Toxicodendron (aka Rhus) radicans

Poison Ivy most commonly grows as vines, but can also appear as a ground cover or small shrub. Vines are covered in brown to reddish hair and can appear pencil thin or larger than a forearm. Leaves are composed of three leaflets and can be small or large, have smooth, lobed or toothed edges, be shiny or dull, and can appear in all shades of green, yellow, and red in the fall. The point where leaflets join often appears reddish. Starting in late spring through the fall, berry clusters will appear yellowish to whitish. A wide variety of animals, insects, amphibians and even reptiles utilize Poison Ivy for food and shelter. Unfortunately for humans, Poison Ivy contains an oil called Urushiol, which can cause an allergic reaction (*in any season!*) if come into contact. Only about 1 out of every 11 people in the U.S. are not allergic to Poison Ivy.

Sweetgum
Liquidambar styraciflua

The Sweetgum tree is easiest to identify by its five-pointed, star-shaped (or crown) leaves. In the fall the leaves turn a deep red color. The fruit, a green spikey ball with a long stem, turns brown through the season and can easily be found on the ground. Sweetgum gets its name from the dried sap that can be chewed like gum.

Jewelweed ✚
Impatiens capensis

Jewelweed is a beautifully delicate plant that grows in moist soils. It's easiest to identify in the spring and summer when the orange and yellow hanging cup-like flowers appear. The plant gets its name from the little silvery and jewel-like beads that appear on the leaves when wet. If you submerge the whole leaf in water it will shimmer silver! However, perhaps the most fun fact about Jewelweed is its natural antidote properties to Poison Ivy. Simply pick a few leaves and stems and mash into a watery pulp between fingers. Then rub the pulp onto areas of skin that came into contact with Poison Ivy.

Common Plantain ✚
Plantago major

Common Plantain is an amazing little common weed. It grows in disturbed sites, on sand, in driveways and throughout lawns. The leaves can be inconspicuous but is easily recognizable once the slender flower stalk appears. The stalk grows throughout the summer and can reach between 2-12 inches tall. Leaves can be chewed and put directly onto bee and insect stings for immediate relief. But please be mindful of where you get the leaves from, and avoid chewing plants near runoff or chemical treated areas.

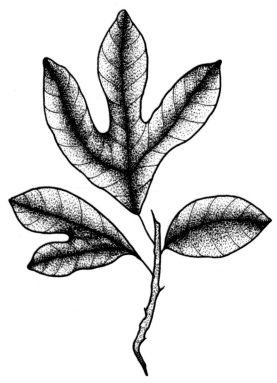

Sassafras
Sassafras albidum

Sassafras is a truly unique tree. It can easily be identified by its leaves. Unlike other trees, Sassafras grows three different shaped leaves which can all usually be found on one plant! The three shapes are ovate (or egg-shaped), two-lobed (resembling a mitten), or three-lobed. Leaf edges are smooth. Native Americans used the leaves, branches, and roots to treat and heal a wide variety of ailments. The roots can be used to make Sassafras tea and was traditionally used to flavor root beer. However, according to the FDA it should not be used because it contains Safrole, a compound found to be carcinogenic.

BIRDS

Pileated Woodpecker
Hylatomus
(Dryocopus) pileatus

The Pileated Woodpecker is the largest woodpecker in our region. It's a large black bird with white stripes along its face and neck, and a striking red crest on top of its head. They are an awesome bird to stumble upon! They can be seen flying low through forest or perched on a dead or decaying tree trunk. Their call is a long, loud bauking that is consistently spaced. Their drumming is fast and loud. Large rectangular shaped holes in trees are evidence of their presence.

Tufted Titmouse
Baeolophus (Parus) bicolor

Tufted Titmice are a bluish-gray color with a white underside. Their sides, just below the wings are a rusty peach color. They have a small crest on the top of their heads with a small black patch above the bill. Their eyes are dark and round. Listen in the spring and you are sure to hear a "pita, pita, pita."

Northern Mockingbird
Mimus polyglottos

Northern Mockingbirds can be real-ly tricky if you are trying to make an ID from sound alone. They appro-priately get their name due to their ability to mimic other bird songs. Northern Mockingbirds are about the size of a robin and are mostly dark gray in color with a lighter un-derside. When they are perched you can often see them bobbing their tail slowly. Another distinctive feature is their white wing patches on both wings easily seen in flight, and white streaks on their outer tail feathers.

101

Red-winged Blackbird
Agelaius phoeniceus

Though the Red-winged Blackbird can be found year-round, it is most prominent during the breeding season in the spring and summer months. Males and females differ greatly in looks. Females are a mix of dull and streaky browns, while the male is black with vibrant red and yellow shoulder tufts. They are commonly found near marshes or fields near water. Listen for a loud and long rolling "r" sound.

Turkey Vulture
Cathartes aura

Often seen soaring with other raptors, Turkey Vultures are easy to spot due to their V-shaped wings in flight. Their black body will contrast with their whitish-gray flight feathers. Also look for a bald red head. Turkey Vultures are extremely common and can be found year-round.

Red-bellied Woodpecker
Melanerpes carolinus

Don't let the name fool you when you are trying to identify the Red-bellied Woodpecker. While the belly is more whitish and pale yellow in color, it's the head that is a distinctive red. The red on the male continues from the brow to the nape, while the female has a small red patch above the bill and on the nape. Their bodies are striped with black and white bars. You can find the Red-bellied Woodpecker year round. Listen for a "churr, churr, churr" with a rolling "r" sound.

Red-eyed Vireo
Vireo olivaceus

The Red-eyed Vireo is commonly heard throughout the summer during its breeding season. Since it mostly stays high in the treetops, you are more likely to hear it rather than see it. They sing throughout the day, so be sure to listen for a bird that sings in short phrases. A common mnemonic is "look up, see me, here I am."

105

Wood Thrush
Hylocichla mustelina

There is no sound more magical than that of the Wood Thrush in the spring forest. Wood Thrushes forage on the ground and are very good at camouflaging themselves. They have a reddish-brown back with a white underside covered in dark, round spots. On a quiet spring or summer morning, listen for their long, flute-like, and whimsical song.

Appendix III
Avoiding Potential Dangers
on the Hike

While thoughtful planning and preparation will greatly reduce your risk of potential hazards on the trail, we have to remember that nature is wild. And though we may not be able to control or predict when, or if, we come into contact with potential dangers, we can reduce the likelihood of such run-ins. Fortunately for us, the habits of the natural living world *are* somewhat predictable. In this section, we will discuss the following potential dangers of hiking in the NYC metro area:

- **Poison Ivy**
- **Ticks**
- **Snakes**
- **Black Bears**
- **Risk of a serious allergic reaction to insect bites or stings**

It is important to note that potentially dangerous species vary from region to region. For this reason, always familiarize yourself with local flora and fauna when you are traveling and hiking in other parts of the country and world.

Poison Ivy

Poison Ivy is extremely common in our area and it can be tricky to identify. It's a vine with a range of appearances that can be found in various habitats. About 85 percent of people are allergic to urushiol, the oil found in poison ivy, poison oak, and poison sumac. The best way to avoid a potential allergic reaction to this oil is to 1) know how to identify the plant, 2) be aware of its growing habits, and 3) learn how to remove the oil from your skin and clothes.

1. Identifying the Plant:
See Appendix II: Field Identification Guide.

2. Be Aware of its Growing Habits:
In our forests Poison Ivy mainly grows as a ground and climbing vine; however, it can sometimes grow as a shrub like you may see along sand dunes at the beach. Poison Ivy commonly thrives along the sides of trails, and many times you will see the vine sprawling up the trunk of a tree. The vine can be as thin as a pencil or as thick as a large forearm. More robust vines will send out branches with leaves, which can sometimes be confused with those of the tree. This is especially true in the summer. When I'm out with a group, I like to point this out. Children like to grab at leaves when they pass by, including little ones in carriers, so it's important to be aware of this growth habit. Poison Ivy vines are always covered in small reddish-brown hairs that help them cling to their support. Based on the location and time of year, the leaves of Poison Ivy may look different. Poison Ivy is deciduous, which means it will drop its leaves in the fall, but the oil remains on the vine which can still cause an allergic reaction. In the spring through the summer, the plant will have three leaflets that join together and meet the

stem—this point of intersection often appears a reddish color. Leaves vary in size and color. They may be dull, shiny, dark green, light green, yellowish, or reddish (in the early spring and fall). Leaf edges may appear lobed, toothed, wavy, or smooth. You may also see whitish berries in late summer to early fall. (Do not touch or eat these berries!)

3. How to Remove Poison Ivy from Your Skin and Clothes:

Urushiol can linger on clothing or gear for a long time. You can also get it from the fur of your animals if they have been in contact with the plant. Making contact with Poison Ivy means that you or an object of yours has rubbed against the plant, allowing the oil to be transferred. Luckily, you have about four hours to remove the oil from your skin before it is absorbed and can cause any harm. If you think you or your child has come into contact with Poison Ivy, the best way to remove the oil is to wash with soap, water, and a washcloth. The washcloth will provide the extra friction needed to remove the oil. Remember that oil is difficult to remove, so be thorough. It's also important to note that an allergic reaction will not appear until a couple of days after exposure. So if you leave the woods feeling itchy, it's not from Poison Ivy.

Ticks

Ticks are arachnids, but only have six legs until they molt into adults and grow eight like their spider "cousins." They can host a number of different viral and bacterial diseases. Ticks are most dangerous to people and pets during the spring and summer (temperatures above 40 degrees), when ticks are most active. Tick eggs are deposited on the ground and develop into larvae. The larvae mostly feed on small mammals, and then hatch into nymphs. Nymphs are dangerous because they are difficult to see (they are about the size of a poppy seed) and can transmit disease. Nymphs live in leaf litter, so you can best avoid them by sticking to the middle of trails.

With that said, some children love to explore in the slightly longer growth along the sides of trails, so be sure to have their pants tucked into their socks to prevent nymphs from crawling under their pants. Also dress your children in lighter clothing to make ticks more visible. There are a wide variety of products on the market to keep ticks off of you and your loved ones, such as essential oils, Deet or Permethrin. Before choosing what is right for your family, you may want to consider the frequency which you plan to use it, and how it could affect your pets. Also it never hurts to speak with your pediatrician.

Ticks have a natural tendency to climb up and snuggle into moist places along waistbands, underwear, bra straps, hairlines, or behind knees. However, they are *opportunists*—I've had to remove a nymph from a child's cheek after only a few minutes of playing in the grass. Be vigilant and always check for ticks after a hike and when bathing. Should you find a tick embedded into the skin, remove it safely, clean the site and treat with an antibacterial. You may want to keep it if you are able to identify it. To best serve you, your doctor will want to know what type of tick you found. For a rule of thumb, it takes about 36 hours for a deer tick (*a.k.a. blacklegged tick*) to transmit Lyme disease. But play it safe and call your doctor or pediatrician and continue to monitor the site. If a bull's eye appears, be sure to call the doctor immediately and seek treatment. For more information on how to remove ticks, see Appendix IV: Useful Resources.

Snakes

Many species of snakes live in the NYC metro area in a variety of habitats. Although there are only two venomous species, the Northern Copperhead and the Timber Rattlesnake, other species of snakes are known to be aggressive or inflict a painful bite if pursued. Snakes have the ability to sense our presence through vibrations in the ground or sound waves passing through the air. Vibrations and sound waves help communicate to parts of the snake's body that something is near. However, some snakes will strike if they are caught off guard or feel threatened. The best way to avoid conflict with a snake is to keep your distance (10 feet is a good rule of thumb). A walking stick may help you feel more comfortable as you can poke around before stepping into a sketchy area. In my experience, the most common snakes you will see are Black Rat Snakes and Eastern Garter Snakes. More rarely, you may see a Northern Water Snake.

While a snake sighting can be exciting, it is not the experience I want to have while hiking with my children, especially once they are exploring on her own. To best avoid snakes, stay away from rocky ledges or exposed rock during the warmest part of the day, during the spring and summer months. Be vigilant when you are hiking along rocky trails that have a lot of nooks and crannies, as snakes like to hide beneath the rocks. With this said, don't let a fear of snakes consume you. Snakes are not out to get us, and for the most part they will try to avoid any interaction with us. Most states have a website dedicated to snakes within their region, which explains what to do if you get bitten by a venomous snake. In the NYC metro area, carrying a snakebite kit is not recommended. For identification and more information about the Northern Copperhead and Timber Rattlesnake, see Appendix 1V: Useful Resources.

Black Bears

Black Bear encounters have been on the rise in the NYC metro area. Though bear sightings are still rare, it is important to know what you can do to minimize your chances of such a run-in. Bears are now more commonly seen in backyards, often near bird feeders or garbage collection areas where they have grown accustomed to feeding on human scraps. However, in the forests, a good bear habitat is one with a lot of coverage or dense vegetation. Black Bears often feed on fruits and nuts, so be especially alert when you are hiking during blueberry and raspberry season.

While you are hiking:

- Avoid wearing heavy perfumes or scents. A bear's sense of smell is far greater than ours.
- Make noises throughout your hike when you are in an active bear area. This will alert the bear and give them time to hide or leave the area. You can use a whistle, your voice, singing, or clapping your hands.
- Carry out what you carry in. Don't leave any food waste or garbage behind. Black Bears that are accustomed to feeding on human scraps can become aggressive towards humans. This is not their natural behavior.

If you see a bear:

- Make sure your children are safe and close to you.
- Be sure the bear has an escape route, and alert it of your presence by talking at a normal level.
- DO NOT RUN from a bear. This will only activate the animal's chase instinct, and they can outrun you. Bears also climb trees, so please don't do that either.
- If a bear approaches, make yourself as big as you can and yell (specifically for Black Bear only). Should the bear stand on its hind legs, it is most likely trying to get a better smell of you. This is NOT aggressive behavior, so again, do not panic and run.
- Never feed a bear or give it your food. This will not deter the bear from following you; rather, it will encourage the animal to follow you further.

Insect Bites or Stings

For an outdoorsy family, I found it very frustrating to get a straight answer from our pediatrician about potential allergic reactions to insect bites or stings. As a parent, I wanted to know my child's odds of having an allergic reaction and how to prepare for one in case they did. What made my pediatrician even more leery to answer my questions was when I asked what I should recommend to my clients, should *their child* get stung and develop an allergic reaction. For both legal and medical reasons, this is highly debated. However, the potential danger when hiking with children who have not been previously exposed to bites or stings is a real concern. My best advice is to speak with your pediatrician about your allergy risk factors, such as your family history. If you have an allergist or a doctor in the family, get their opinions as well. Determine what you and your family are comfortable with. If you feel your child is low-risk, carrying a liquid antihistamine may be all you need to treat hives or welts (babies will not be able to chew a pill). Or, you may feel more secure carrying an epinephrine auto-injector. Just be sure you know how to use it. In the case of anaphylactic shock, you will not have much time. You will need to call 911 immediately, use the auto-injector, and get to help right away. In the case of an emergency, it is better to use an auto-injector, even when the dosage is high for an infant.

What might all this mean for your hike? Hike for shorter distances in the warmer months, when insects are more active. In case of an emergency, you will need to seek medical attention immediately. In the most severe cases, you need to seek help within a 15 minute window. For these reasons, talk to your doctors and come up with a solution that you are comfortable with, so that you can feel confident and in control.

---

[1]American Academy of Allergy, Asthma and Immunology, 2017

Appendix IV
Useful Resources

Cornell Lab of Ornithology: www.birds.cornell.edu/

Fieldbook: The BSA's Manual of Advanced Skills for Outdoor Travel, Adventure, and Caring for the Land by Boy Scouts of America (2004)

Minimal impact fire building: www.lnt.org (Leave No Trace)

New Jersey Department of Environmental Protection: www.nj.gov/dep

New York-New Jersey Trail Conference: https://www.nynjtc.org/

New York State Department of Environmental Conservation: https://www.dec.ny.gov/

Pennsylvania Department of Conservation and Natural Resources: http://www.dcnr.pa.gov/

Snakes of New Jersey: http://www.state.nj.us/dep/fgw/ensp/pdf/snake_broch07.pdf

Snakes of New York: http://www.esf.edu/pub-prog/brochure/snakes/snakes.htm

Tick Removal: www.cdc.gov/ticks/removing_a_tick.html

Author Bio

Lori LaBorde is Founder of NYC Adventure Moms, a community-building hiking organization that honors the female spirit and strength of motherhood, and encourages families to spend time outdoors with their little ones.

Lori holds a Bachelor of Science in Wildlife Management from the University of New Hampshire and a Master of Arts in Teaching Biology from New York University. As a naturalist, science educator, and licensed NYSDEC hiking guide, she has designed and implemented environmental curricula for both formal and informal educational settings, including training programs in safety and plant and animal identification.

In addition to her studies and work in Tanzania, Lori has worked on various volunteer projects in Costa Rica, New York State, Queens NY, and throughout New Jersey. She currently serves as the Operations Director for The South Mountain Conservancy of Essex County, New Jersey.

Lori lives with her husband, two children, and cat in Maplewood, NJ, finding adventures and balance through her experiences in nature.

Notes from the Field

_____

_____

_____

_____

_____

_____

_____

_____

_____

_____

_____

_____

_____

_____

_____

_____

_____

_____

_____

_____

_____

_____

_____

Notes from the Field

Notes from the Field

Notes from the Field

Notes from the Field

Notes from the Field

Notes from the Field

Notes from the Field

Notes from the Field